HELP
YOUR
CHILD
DE-STRESS

Substantial discounts on bulk quantities of Summersdale books are available to corporations, professional associations and other organizations. For details contact general enquiries: telephone: +44 (0) 1243 771107 or email: enquiries@summersdale.com.

HELP
YOUR
CHILD
DE-STRESS

101 Ways to Ease Worries and Encourage Calm

VICKI VRINT

Disclaimer

Neither the author nor the publisher can be held responsible for any loss or claim arising out of the use, or misuse, of the suggestions made herein. None of the views or suggestions in this book is intended to replace medical opinion from a doctor. If you have concerns about your health or that of a child in your care, please seek professional advice.

CONTENTS

How to Use This Book

If you're concerned that your child is suffering from stress and worries a lot, this book is here to help.

Drawing on tried and trusted counselling techniques – such as cognitive behavioural therapy (CBT) – it explores practical ways to deal with the symptoms and causes of stress. The book takes a holistic approach, including tips to promote relaxation and mindfulness, and to improve your child's well-being. There's no one-size-fits-all solution to dealing with your child's stress, so try out a few ideas and pick the ones that appeal most to you and your child.

Stress levels may peak at different stages in your child's development – pre-schoolers often suffer from separation anxiety, for example, while teenagers may be susceptible to social stress or can be affected by the pressure of exams. *Help Your Child De-Stress* includes advice and support for you and your child whatever their age.

INTRODUCTION

Stress is something we all experience – it's a natural reaction to challenging situations – but for children it can be particularly upsetting, as they may not have the skills to handle or articulate their feelings. Recent studies have found that one in four children aged between 5 and 16 show some evidence of mental ill health, including anxiety and depression.* If your child is stressed or going through a difficult situation, please try not to worry: there's so much you can do to support them, and being ready and willing to help is a great start.

This book includes plenty of tips to help you and your child tackle challenging moments together. By teaching them to cope when times are tough, you'll be giving them valuable skills they'll rely on later in life too.

* Source: Office of National Statistics, 2016

CHAPTER 1

Spotting the Signs of Stress

We all experience stress in different ways, but there are some common symptoms that you can look out for in your child. This chapter discusses these different signs, how to identify them and effective ways to alleviate them. There are also some tips on how to talk to your child about stress and help them to make sense of their feelings.

Understand stress

It's worth taking a moment to explain what we mean by stress – it's the feeling we have when we are under pressure. Everyone reacts differently to stress – for some it can be motivating – but if your child feels unable to cope and the pressure is too much, stress can become a problem. Stress is usually a fairly immediate reaction to a pressured situation, but that's not always the case. If your child has experienced a challenging situation or life change, stress symptoms can develop up to a month or so later.

Look for changes in behaviour

A change in your child's behaviour can be one of the first signs of stress. Your usually cheerful child may appear more irritable and angry, or shy away from trying new things or carrying out their usual activities. Perhaps they are not sleeping well or have become picky with their food, or have started sucking their thumb or twirling their hair. Older children might adopt new behaviours to cope with stress, such as disappearing into the virtual world of a computer game, becoming withdrawn and even experimenting with stimulants such as alcohol. If any of these changes resonate with you, try not to worry – there's plenty you can do to help your child feel safe again, and there is support available to help you tackle serious issues.

CHECK FOR PHYSICAL SYMPTOMS

It may seem surprising, but stress can cause all sorts of physical symptoms, including:

- **Stomach pains**
- **Headaches**
- **Nausea**
- **Dizziness**
- **Chest pains**
- **Loss of appetite**
- **Lethargy**
- **Needing the toilet more frequently**
- **Fidgeting**

It's always best to check with a medical professional to rule out any medical causes for these symptoms, but if there are none, stress could be at the root of these problems.

TIP
4

Think about cognitive changes

Stress often affects the way our brains work, so you may notice that your child is thinking differently or reacting differently to the challenges of day-to-day life. Look out for:

- Poor concentration

- Negative thoughts

- Forgetfulness

- Nightmares

- Low self-esteem

- A feeling of being overwhelmed

- Crying more frequently

- Irritability and anger

Take heart if your child is experiencing any of these things: when you tackle stress, with the right support, these symptoms will improve and can be eliminated completely.

Try talking

Asking your child about changes in their behaviour can seem like a tall order for both of you. What's most important is that your child doesn't feel pressured into talking. Introduce the topic while you're doing a calming activity together, such as going for a walk or baking a cake, rather than having a face-to-face discussion. Ask your child whether they're worried about anything and tell them that you're always there to listen and help if you can. If your child does open up immediately, remember to listen rather than rushing to offer advice – let them lead the conversation. If they don't want to talk, don't worry: it may take time and a more creative approach to discover what's wrong.

Observe their actions

Remember that some children may simply be unable to tell you how they're feeling. They may be too young to understand what stress means; they may not realize that they're suffering from it, or they may find it hard to express themselves in words. A child who has just started school, for example, may not realize that the reason they feel anxious is that they're comparing themselves with their classmates. A teenager may feel reluctant to discuss a difficult situation that's worrying them at home. Never try to force an uncommunicative child to tell you what's wrong, as this will exacerbate their stress. Look instead at how they might be showing you that they need help via their actions, such as shutting themselves away or being angry. Your goal isn't necessarily to get your child to speak, it's to understand and support them.

TRY MOOD TRACKING

Using a mood tracker can help you keep tabs on your child's emotions and pinpoint any stressful moments during the week. You can use an app for this, but it's really simple to put together a chart at home. Draw a column for each day of the week, with space to record their morning, afternoon and evening mood, or simply note one mood a day if it's easier. Encourage your child to complete the tracker using different emojis to represent different moods. (You could offer them an incentive to do this, if necessary.) This will help your child to focus on how they're feeling. Look out for patterns to help you identify stress triggers: if your child feels worried every Tuesday evening, for example, perhaps something they do every Wednesday is difficult for them; or perhaps they become anxious any time you're away or working late.

Explain stress

It can help your child to deal with stress if they understand how it feels and what can cause it. You'll need to pick an age-appropriate approach for your child, but a simple definition is a good place to start. For example, "Stress is something we all experience when we're facing a tricky situation – it happens when you feel worried or uncomfortable about something." You could discuss how stress can affect us physically and how it can change our behaviour. Talking about a favourite story or cartoon where a character faces a stressful situation can help or you could use role-play so that you're not discussing your child directly.

Explore stress

You can help children explore what stress means to them by asking them some questions – they can either write or draw their answers, or you can talk through them together. Here are a few ideas to start you off:

- **"What do you think of when you hear the word 'stress'?"**

- **"What happens when you feel stressed?"**

- **"Where in your body do you feel stress?"**

- **"What might make you worried?"**

- **"What can you do to feel better?"**

Investigate further

Sometimes the signs of stress may not be immediately obvious, but if you feel something's not right, take time to think through what's different about your child's behaviour and mood. It might help to write down your thoughts. List any life changes your child has experienced – such as moving house, changing schools, the arrival of a new sibling or a bereavement – could there be a link? (Remember, stress reactions can be delayed.) It may be worth chatting to family members or your child's teacher to see if they've picked up on anything lately. Above all, trust your instinct – if you sense something's off, it's worth investigating further.

CHAPTER 2

The Causes
of Stress

It's not always easy to work out what's worrying your child. This chapter describes how you can explore what's at the root of your child's stress. It looks at some of the common causes, along with ways to make these situations a little less stressful for everyone concerned.

TAKE A CHILD'S POINT OF VIEW

It's easy for us adults to forget that childhood can be a pretty stressful experience, so it can be useful to take a moment to put yourself in your child's shoes. They may be:

- **Feeling pressure from parents, teachers, friends and the media to look, perform and behave in a particular way.**

- **Coping with the physical changes of puberty and experiencing more intense feelings.**

- **Trying to work out who they are as a person.**

- **Wanting to fit in with — or impress — others.**

- **Feeling inadequate.**

- **Dealing with changes in their home life, such as parents splitting up or moving house.**

Bearing all this in mind can help you to understand how intense your child's experiences may feel.

Listen actively

Active listening is a technique used by therapists to encourage a child to open up about their feelings. When your child is communicating with you, respond by using body language to show you are listening and understanding. When they have had their say, paraphrase what they have said and show empathy by saying things like:

"I hear what you're saying and I can see why that would make you feel worried."

"How does your body feel when you're experiencing these thoughts?"

Communicate without speaking

If your child isn't open to big discussions, they might like to write a letter, poem or email to tell you how they're feeling – drawing a picture could work well too. Taking this approach will allow your child to think about what they want to say and how they want to say it in their own time. They may also be worried about how you will react and may feel happier about you reading their worries while they're not in the room, then chatting about them afterward. And, of course, texting is second nature to most children and will allow them to take control of the conversation in a familiar way.

Take them seriously

Younger children may fret about things that seem trivial to us, but take their concerns seriously and listen to their worries. They may be afraid of the noisy monster in the radiator, or heartbroken because they've just found out they'll never get to ride a unicorn, but the fear or heartbreak they're experiencing are very real to them. Whatever your child's age, resist the urge to brush away their concerns — don't tell them "It's nothing". Try to see things from their point of view and aim to comfort them calmly without validating their fears. You don't need to agree with your child, but you can still affirm and empathize with them.

MAKE THEM FEEL "GOOD ENOUGH"...

Before we look at some specific causes of stress, let's discuss one common theme that underpins many of them: not feeling good enough. This is a huge issue for children and it's at the heart of a lot of childhood stress. Whether it's unrealistic expectations at school – not everyone can come top of the class! – or unrealistic comparisons with celebrities and vloggers, children are often left feeling inadequate, a feeling they can carry forward through life. As parents we're in pole position to counteract these pressures – and to make sure we're not contributing to them without realizing it!

... by building their confidence

Building confident and resilient children is one of the most important ways you can combat stress and ensure they're able to handle the trickier times that come their way. Here are some suggestions to help you do it:

- Praise your child for effort rather than achievement.

- Don't compare their performance with that of other children or siblings.

- Remember that even "funny" remarks can be taken to heart.

- Make them feel valued by giving them your undivided attention at some point every day.

- Love the things they love and encourage their enthusiasms.

- Encourage independence.

- Respect their opinions.

- Remind them that they're more than "good enough"... they're amazing! (And so are you.)

Avoid overscheduling

While it's wonderful for your child to try new hobbies, be wary of signing them up to too many activities. If your child wants to join every club going, encourage their enthusiasm but be practical about what you can all achieve. The pressure of getting to the right place, at the right time, with the right equipment can be stressful for everyone if you try to do it too many times a week! Remember, too, that school is very tiring whatever your child's age and they may like to relax at weekends, rather than taking on other timetabled activities. (They can still spend time outside, of course, but try a walk to the park or a ball game in the garden instead of a day-long hike.)

Help them to wind down after school

We'll look at some specific school stressors in the following pages, but if your child finds day-to-day school life challenging, it helps to make their home life as comforting as possible. Get a regular routine in place. If they need to burn off energy after school, send them outside with a ball or give them some gaming time. If they just need quiet time to process the day, let them listen to a podcast or read a book with a warm drink. Include a moment to chat one-to-one about their day when they're ready to do so.

EASE EXAM STRESS

Every year, child-support charities receive thousands of calls from young people struggling to cope with the pressure of exams. There are many ways to support your child at exam time:

- **Help them to devise a revision plan that includes regular breaks for fun and exercise.**

- **Explore different methods of revising that suit your child.**

- **Suggest that they find a study buddy, so that they can support and motivate each other.**

- **Give them a clear and quiet space to work.**

- **Make learning fun, with treats or rewards.**

- **Make sure they're eating well and getting a good night's sleep.**

- **Offer some perspective so they don't feel their future is entirely dependent on their results.**

Tackle bullying

If your child is reluctant to go to school, complains of illness to avoid going in, or comes home with spoiled belongings, it's possible they're being bullied. Try to teach your child to deal with minor bullying themselves – remind them that bullies are often seeking attention and that simply ignoring them or practising a quick response may be enough to stop the problem. If the bullying is more serious or sustained, keep a record of what's happened and speak to your school's leadership team. It may take some patience but by keeping the lines of communication open you should be able to tackle it together. There's extra support available for you online – anti-bullying charities have websites that offer plenty of information and help on dealing with this tricky issue.

Support their friendships

From falling out with friends to hanging out with the wrong crowd, friendships can be a minefield, but there are ways you can help your child build strong bonds and make wise decisions about the company they keep. Help them to identify what's important in friendship – honesty, loyalty, trust, kindness and an element of fun – and make sure they realize they should look for these qualities in their friends, as well as offer them.

If your child is shy and struggling to make friends, help them to develop an interest that could provide common ground with classmates, and host an out-of-school meet-up to get things started. If they fall out with a friend, help your child to get a sense of perspective and discuss a solution together. Role-playing different scenarios can help too.

Deal with social media stress

Social media is a great tool, but it does open your child up to a new type of stress, whether that's the pressure to portray a perfect life, have a popular online presence or to deal with the negative remarks people often express online. Remind your child that social media presents an "airbrushed" version of the real world, and that people often post things thoughtlessly or may not mean them in a negative way. Research which apps you're happy for your child to use and make sure they're clued up about online safety. Building their confidence with plenty of real-world distractions is a great way to counteract social media stress in your child.

DEAL WITH ONLINE BULLIES

If your child is spending more time checking their phone than usual, or becomes upset after doing so, they may be encountering negativity online. Around 20 per cent of children experience online bullying*, but there are subtler stressors to look out for too: feeling left out from other friends' activities, for example, or feeling inferior when others show off new purchases. Redirect your child's attention from these worries by encouraging them to take part in real-world activities they enjoy. If they're experiencing more serious online stress – unpleasant texts or negative comments on social media platforms – keep screenshots of what's taken place and report the offenders to the service provider. It may help to link to your child's social media account and monitor things from there. Bear in mind, too, that your child may make negative comments about others, so make sure that they realize the importance of kind words and the damage that online trolling can do.

* Source: www.internetmatters.org

Discourage sibling rivalry

All families experience sibling rivalry – studies show that on average children argue three to six times an hour!* – but you can minimize stress between siblings with a consistent approach:

- Give your children the same amount of attention and praise, even though their interests and achievements may be different.

- Don't compare them with one another.

- Promote fun bonding activities.

- If your children are fighting over an item, take it away.

- Set rules together, including consequences for bad behaviour – and follow through with them.

- If you can't decide who was in the wrong during an argument, give everyone the same consequence.

If all else fails, take heart: sibling rivalry teaches your children how to handle disagreements and deal with big emotions in later life.

* Source: "Administering Justice in the Family", *Journal of Family Psychology*, 1994

Help them to cope with change

Changes to your family set-up can be tricky for children to negotiate. Parents separating, a house move or change of school, or the arrival of a new sibling can leave children feeling anxious as all that's safe and familiar is swept away. How you handle these situations will depend on your child, but preparation and lots of reassurance are essential. Make sure that your child knows what to expect and ask them about any specifics that may be worrying them. For house or school moves, visiting the new area (if possible) will help. Age-appropriate books that discuss these issues can also be very useful.

Help them to cope with loss

If your child is facing the loss of a loved one, you may feel powerless to take away their stress, but there are practical things you can do. It is essential for your child to be able to talk about their feelings, so communicate as honestly as possible without overwhelming them. It's important they know it's normal to experience a range of emotions, which come and go without warning. Reassure them that they are loved and safe. If you're dealing with the loss of an elderly relative, it can be helpful to explain to them that you belong to a different generation to Grandma, for example, so that they are less likely to worry about losing you too. Making a memory box together can be a comfort. There are also many charities with information online to help you navigate this difficult area.

HELP THEM TO DEAL WITH DIFFICULT NEWS

From time to time, children are exposed to news stories that can be upsetting, confusing or downright scary. Even if your home is a news-free zone, social media and school pals will spread – and often exaggerate – what's going on in the wider world. For younger children, the best approach is to keep things simple and reassure them that they're safe. If older children seem affected by bad news stories, explore their thoughts or feelings to see where their worries lie first, then you can address any specific concerns. Listen and reassure them that their feelings are normal. It may be worth buying a children's newspaper or checking out an online children's news service together to get a balanced and child-friendly approach to what's happening.

Be aware of body image

We're all familiar with curated images in the media promoting unrealistic expectations of how we should look, so it's easy to see how children can grow up with negative feelings about their appearance and low self-worth. Limit the amount of time your child is exposed to these images and make sure they realize they aren't realistic. It's important to avoid making negative remarks about appearance in front of your children. Don't talk about trying to lose weight, for example, but do talk about exercising to be strong and eating well to feel healthy. Even young children can pick up on negative body image, and if they see you criticizing your own figure, they may start to look for flaws in themselves. One study of childcare workers, for example, showed that 24 per cent of them had heard three- to five-year-olds making negative remarks about their own bodies.*

* Source: PACEY, 2016

CHAPTER 3

De-Stressing Strategies

There are plenty of different ways you can tackle your child's stress. Talking is important, so this chapter includes tips on effective ways to do this. There are also exercises you can do to release pent-up feelings, techniques to try to help your child put things in perspective and even some ideas for things you can prepare ahead – such as putting together a de-stress plan and a de-stress pack – to help you both cope when stress strikes.

Have chat check-ins

Teach your children that talking about things makes us feel better. It's nice to have a weekly family chat where everyone can discuss their activities and concerns, so that talking about feelings becomes a part of everyday life. For a stressed child, though, a regular quiet moment together, which could begin with a calming ritual such as making a drink or lighting a candle, can help your child to relax and enjoy some quiet conversation with you. You may not discuss their worries directly, but having a regular check-in and safe place to do it will be a reassurance and a comfort. Pick the time of day that suits your child best and have your check-in together then.

Learn to listen

If your child is sharing their worries, let them speak without interruption. Don't talk over them or leap in with advice – remember the discussion is about them. Make sure they feel able to talk without judgement. When they've finished speaking, empathize and show that you've understood how they're feeling by reflecting it back: "That must feel so frustrating to you...", for example. If you do have advice, ask if your child would like to hear it before sharing. And, if your children say things that you find hurtful to hear, try not to take it personally: remember all children have a very child-centric point of view.

BE MINDFUL OF WHAT YOU SAY

How you respond to your child's worries can have a big impact on their feelings. You need to show your child that you take their feelings seriously but help to give them some perspective at the same time. Don't dismiss your child's fears, laugh them off or say they're being silly – "That's nothing to worry about!" And try to avoid labelling your child by saying things like "Oh, you're just shy". A good approach is: "I can understand that must feel very upsetting/stressful/frustrating to you", then see if together you can think of one practical thing you can do to improve things.

Work on a de-stress plan

By teaching your child what to do if they start to feel stressed, you'll be helping them to break the stress cycle – and giving them a coping strategy that will set them up for life.

Younger children can learn to stop, take slow calming breaths and focus on a positive word, thought or image. Practise this with them, choosing a focal point that suits them best – they might choose to imagine the sun shining brightly or to picture their favourite teddy, or they might choose a word to think about such as "calm" or "safe".

Older children can extend this by learning to put their situation in perspective (see p. 107) and then thinking of the very first thing they need to do to move forward. Having something practical to do will help them feel in control of the situation. Show them how to choose something small, manageable and immediate, to make their situation seem less intimidating.

STOP > BREATHE > THINK > ACT

Encourage them to use affirmations

Affirmations are short positive statements that help us to focus on different aspects of our life. If we repeat them frequently, our brains come to accept them as fact – which is why they can be an effective way of tackling stress. If you teach your child to pause and repeat "I am calm" to themselves when they feel stressed, they'll soon feel calmer, thanks to the repetition and focus. Over time their general stress levels will lower too. You can change your affirmation to suit the situation – "I am confident" or "I can do it", for example.

Show them how to let it out

Big emotions can be difficult for children to handle, and stress can build up and cause some pretty explosive behaviour. Help your child to vent their feelings in a safe and appropriate way. Some ideas for how to do this include: shouting – it's best to go somewhere remote for this! – going for a run, having a cry, scribbling in a notebook, singing, listening to loud music, or doing any energetic outdoor exercise. You could have a boxing session with pads and gloves, or get your child to push against a wall for ten seconds or so – tensing, then relaxing their muscles will release calming feel-good hormones.

SEND STRESS PACKING

Help your child to de-stress by doing something to symbolize getting rid of their worries. They could write down what's worrying them on pieces of paper and put them in a worry jar, for example. Otherwise, they could scrunch their paper worries into a ball and throw them away, or tear them up. A chalkboard for writing down and erasing worries is another good option, or they could paint them on the patio or pavement in water and watch them disappear. Alternatively, visualizations work well for some children, so you could suggest they imagine putting their worries in a big box, nailing down the lid and firing it off into space.

Teach them belly breathing

Learning to focus on our breathing is a great mindfulness exercise for everyone, which is immediately calming. Practising a daily breathing ritual can be a nice part of your child's bedtime routine: just sit quietly together and breathe in to a count of four, then out to a count of four, feeling your body relax as you do so. Try balancing a teddy on your child's belly and encourage them to watch it rise and fall as they breathe. See if they can slow Teddy down. (Slower, deeper breaths send signals to your nervous system telling it to relax, thereby lowering stress levels.)

Calm them down with repetition

Studies have shown that repetitive movements have a calming effect on us, both physically and mentally. (This is why many crafting activities or even some chores can help us to relax.) For a stressed child, a simple activity such as throwing and catching a ball, or throwing it from hand to hand, can be effective in helping them to relax. Jumping on a trampoline, drumming, clapping slowly, painting or kneading putty or dough are all good options.

Create a de-stress pack

Preparing a pack for your child to use when they're feeling stressed is really effective. For younger children, you could include a teddy, a favourite book, a tactile toy and something that plays calming music. A worry-eater toy is also a nice idea – children write down their worries and zip them away in the toy's mouth ready for you to remove overnight. Older children may appreciate a pamper kit, which could contain things like bubble wrap to pop, a blanket scented with essential oils, a de-stress journal, or sports and games items that help them unwind. They could have a de-stress playlist on their phone too.

MAKE A SAFE SPACE OR DEN

Even as an adult it's appealing to have a special corner to relax in, but creating a safe space or den for your child can really help to lower their stress levels. Pop-up tents and tipis are lovely and can be used indoors or outside, but you don't need to buy anything elaborate. Help your child to construct a den with a sheet or blanket, or screen off a corner by adjusting the layout of your furniture. Fill their safe space with cushions and blankets and help your child to decorate it with positive pictures or photos of family and friends.

Show them how to use counting to calm down

Counting gives the mind something to focus on and your child a chance to compose themselves in stressful moments. For younger children, make a habit of counting to five with them whenever they feel angry or stressed. (You could ask them to count five deep breaths, to make this even more calming.) This gives any volatile feelings a chance to settle and can stop your child from acting in anger. Older children can focus on counting down backwards from 50 or 100. By the time they've reached their goal, they should feel calmer and have a better perspective on things.

Don't always try to fix it

If you've identified a definite cause of stress, it's natural to want to wade in and sort out your child's problems for them, but this may not be the best plan. Obviously if your child is very distressed you'll need to do all you can to help, but for more minor worries – a misunderstanding with a friend, for example – don't promise to fix the problem for them. Instead, talk through their situation together and discuss the best way to sort it out. The amount of help they'll need in doing this will depend on their age – you may need to give younger children a little more support. Teaching your child to problem-solve these situations is an essential skill for later life.

Talk about what they can — and can't — control

Teaching your child that there are some things in life they just can't change should help to reduce their stress levels. To explain, you could talk about how you can't stop the rain from falling, for example, but you *can* decide what to do about the weather instead: such as packing an umbrella or deciding to jump in some puddles! Alternatively, draw a circle and help your child to write inside it things we can control in life (being kind, trying our best and so on) and put the things we can't control (the past, other people's thoughts about us and so on) on the outside.

HELP THEM FACE THEIR FEARS

If your child tries something they perceive as scary, they're more than likely to discover that it's not so stressful after all — fear often comes from the unknown. Encouraging them to take gentle steps toward their challenges — and praising them for their bravery — will really give your child a boost. (Trying new things also creates new neural pathways in the brain, which helps it to grow and become more adept at problem-solving.) Your child can then look back on these victories when they're facing new challenges and remember how they conquered them. Children who learn to handle stress will become more positive, happier, stronger adults better prepared to cope with life.

Know when to get help

Don't forget that there's plenty of professional help available if you and your child are struggling to cope. Generally, if your child's stress is severe and doesn't show signs of improvement or is impacting on their well-being, it's a good idea to seek help. You can try the pastoral team at school or your doctor, who can refer you to a counsellor or local support services. There are several really useful websites with information on all aspects of childhood stress. You could try:

- www.apa.org
- www.kidshealth.org
- www.mind.org.uk
- www.themix.org.uk
- www.youngminds.org.uk

CHAPTER 4

Mood Boosters

There are plenty of simple things you can do with your child to cheer them up, whether they need a bit of a morale boost, a break from school work or a distraction from their worries. If you have a go at these tips together, you'll feel the benefits too. Most of them are free to try out and all of them are fun!

Laugh!

Laughter is one of the simplest and speediest ways to boost your mood. Laughing triggers the release of mood-boosting endorphins in the brain, and it also activates and then releases the stress response, which leaves us feeling calmer. So watch something funny with your child, make up nonsense rhymes, have a tickling contest, dress up in silly clothes or speak in squeaky voices, and maybe invent a child-friendly "rude" word or two – "muffins" has great comedy value, for example. Be sure to include some laughter every day and you'll all feel the benefits.

Encourage them to spend time with friends

Fun with friends never fails to cheer your child, so encourage them to have regular meet-ups — or arrange these for them if they're younger. (If your child finds friendship-building tricky, there's plenty you can do to support them, such as helping them find a hobby they can share with others, or role-playing conversations.) Friendship gatherings don't need to be expensive or flashy — a movie night or gaming session with a few snacks and drinks is a good option, or head outside for a picnic in the park. And remember you don't need to wait for a birthday party to include some games as part of the fun.

TAKE THEM OUTDOORS – OFTEN!

Spending time outside is one of the most enjoyable and effective ways of de-stressing – and it's essential for all of us. Plenty of studies have shown the positive effect that time spent outdoors engaging with nature can have, and of course there are plenty of fun ways for your child to do this. Bike rides, outdoor sports, a scavenger hunt or a nature walk are great, but a simple picnic in the yard, an outdoor drawing session with chalks or a stroll to the shops will be enough to get your child interacting with the elements and feeling calmer and happier.

Help them to focus on the details

Science has shown that studying the patterns in nature – called fractals – has such a calming effect on the brain that it can reduce stress levels by up to 60 per cent.* Find a practical activity that helps your child to focus on the details of the natural world. Spend some time together looking for the patterns in clouds, sketching leaves and flowers or making a bark rubbing or two. Why not collect some leaves or other natural treasures on your next walk, and then help your child make a collage with them when you get home.

* Source: "Fun with Fractals?", *Psychology Today*, 2012

Get them to look after an animal

The mood-boosting effects of spending time with animals are well documented, and caring for creatures can be very therapeutic. The responsibility and focus of looking after another living thing provide a brilliant distraction from everyday worries. You might not want to commit to keeping a pet yourself, but you're sure to have friends or family who will let you spend time with theirs. Older children may be able to volunteer at an animal shelter or walk a neighbour's dog, while little ones will love a visit to a farm trail. And – of course – everyone knows that YouTube videos of animals provide endless smiles and laughter.

Play!

Never underestimate the power of play — even adults benefit from indulging in non-productive, fun activities. Set aside regular playtimes with your child and throw yourself into whichever game they love best. For imaginary play, let them take the lead, or plan a mood-boosting play break with a game of Grandmother's Footsteps, Marco Polo or Hunt the Thimble, or devise an indoor obstacle course. For reluctant teens, you could use some stealth play tactics: take a trip to the beach where stone-stacking, paddling and wave-dodging will tempt even the most self-conscious of players.

GET THEM INTO A REGULAR EXERCISE HABIT

Exercise is a brilliant – and essential – option for boosting your child's mood: it releases endorphins, it keeps them fit and if you choose something they love it will be lots of fun too. If your child enjoys sports, team games can be exciting and help them build friendships and self-confidence. Or, for some one-to-one time at home, you could try skipping-rope challenges, hopscotch or learning some martial arts moves. You can include exercise in their routine with a walk or bike ride to school, and some active chore time, such as sweeping leaves or vacuuming the house – it's not quite so much fun, but it will leave them with a great sense of achievement!

Encourage them to try yoga

Yoga provides a combined hit of mindfulness and relaxation. It will also improve your child's coordination and concentration. Children's yoga classes often involve storytelling and can be very rewarding, but there are plenty of ways to try yoga for free. YouTube tutorials are a great place to start, or simply look up a few of the basic animal-based poses (Cat, Cobra, Lion) and weave these into a story for your child to act out. Even the easiest position of all — Legs Up the Wall pose — is fun, and if you do it together once a day, you'll get a chance to chat one-to-one while relaxing.

Sing!

Singing makes us happy: not only are there the physical benefits of deeper breaths, which boost our oxygen intake, and the release of those endorphins again, but when your child is concentrating on making music their mind is distracted from everyday worries. You could have a sing-along playlist for the car, encourage older children to perform their own versions of their favourite tracks for you or get little ones to sing along to the latest movie soundtrack. You can discover new tunes together by learning some campfire songs along with the actions, or by trying a karaoke app.

Help them to help others

There are many benefits to be had from helping others. Studies show that our mood is boosted by altruistic actions, and it's a nice idea to teach your child the importance of showing kindness to others from an early age. They can start in small ways, by looking out for someone who needs a friend at school, picking up litter or donating to a food bank or homeless shelter. They'll soon start to develop ideas of their own: perhaps they could bake gifts; drop off a neighbour's groceries or walk their dog; or write to a relative who's living alone. Volunteering helps children to build confidence too, and they'll love the feeling that they've made a difference. Teenagers can often help with sorting donations in charity shops, for example, or with more practical work, such as conservation projects. Younger children can help you to fundraise or put together care packages for those in need.

INSPIRE THEM TO GET CREATIVE

Creative hobbies reduce stress and improve mood, and there are so many options to choose from to tempt your child. Pick something they find absorbing, whether it's an art-based activity, such as painting, or a different creative outlet, such as learning an instrument, jewellery making, baking, drama or creative writing. You can get lots of ideas for age-appropriate creative projects online, but simply having a stash of paper and drawing ideas to hand will be enough to set your children off on a creative session. You could get young ones to design their favourite cake, invent an alien or plan their dream bedroom or outfit. Older children could experiment with different styles of drawing, create cartoons of celebrities or try their hand at origami.

Play to their strengths

Doing the things we're good at leaves us feeling accomplished and happy, so whatever your child shows promise in, give them the opportunity to put it into practice when they can. Everyone has something they excel at, but if your child hasn't found their niche yet, let them have fun trying out some different activities – without overburdening them, of course – until they discover "their thing". They'll gain confidence as they develop their skills and will get a real buzz out of feeling like a pro, which is a perfect antidote to those moments when they're feeling stressed or lacking in confidence.

Have a hug

Simple but immediately effective, a hug will lower blood pressure, boost the immune system and leave your child feeling happier. Older children can love a hug as much as a toddler, although they may not admit it! If you or your child find it difficult to express feelings verbally, a hug can work wonders. If your child isn't a hugger, they might still like to snuggle together to watch TV or read a story, or you may find that a comforting squeeze on the arm works for them. Even during tempestuous teenage moments, you can find a way to show your love and support. My daughter and I link little fingers until it's safe to hug again!

Pay a compliment

Positive words brighten anyone's day. Praising your child for trying their best will give them a real boost. You could leave sticky notes with positive messages on them around the house for your child to find or text older children saying how proud you are of them – they'll feel better for it, even if they don't acknowledge it! Don't overdo the praise, though, and make sure it's genuine. You could pick a specific detail you like about a drawing they've done, for example, or praise the effort they've put into something.

DANCE IT OUT

Put together a playlist of your child's favourite songs and have a dance around the house – the sillier the better. Incorporate household objects as props, imagine you're in a musical and going for the big finish, conga round the kitchen or have a go at recreating a dance routine from YouTube. You'll enjoy all the benefits of music, laughter and exercise in one go. This is a mood booster that never fails – just move any family heirlooms out of the way before you start!

Teach them to practise gratitude

If you teach your child to focus on the things they're grateful for, you'll bring positivity into their day and beyond into their adult life. People who focus on the good things in life tend to achieve more and feel much less stressed. Many studies have shown the positive effects of this, but one in particular shows that practising gratitude causes changes in the brain that allow us to perform better.* The good news is that focusing on positives is something we can train our brains to do with practice. Toward the end of the day – on the journey home from school, perhaps, or at bedtime – chat with your child about the event, person or thing they're most grateful for and talk a little about why these things are important to them. Your child may even like to draw or write about their favourite things in life in a journal.

* Source: "The Grateful Heart: The Psychophysiology of Appreciation", 2004

CHAPTER 5

Forming Positive Habits and Routines

As a parent you're in a great position to help your child adopt positive habits that can last a lifetime, and which will bring them continued health and happiness. This chapter provides tips on how to do this and also on how to set up some useful routines. Routines are a really effective way of creating a calm and positive environment at home. It's much easier for children to face the worries of the outside world if they have a comforting and predictable routine at home.

Encourage them to eat for good health

Eating a healthy balanced diet is one of the most important habits you can help your child to adopt. Teach your child about the important food groups and to avoid sugars, sweeteners and other additives – such as nitrates and MSG – that can affect mood and sleep. Lead by example, picking fresh, non-processed options and including lots of colourful fruits and veggies in your diet. Take your child grocery shopping, get them on board with food prep and try to avoid making mealtimes a battlefield. If all else fails, look up some stealth veggie-camouflaging tricks online.

NOTE: Some nutrients are essential for good mental health. In particular, it's vital to get enough omega 3 fatty acids (found in nuts, seeds and fish), which help with brain function and development, and vitamin B (found in whole grains, meat, eggs, legumes and leafy greens). Low levels of vitamin B are linked to depression and anxiety, and we cannot store it in the body, so try to ensure that your child eats vitamin B-rich foods regularly. If your child makes a sudden change to their diet, look out for any effects on their mood. You may also consider supplementing these nutrients in their diet.

KEEP THEM HYDRATED

Staying hydrated is just as important as eating a well-balanced diet. Dehydration can cause headaches and lethargy, and increase the levels of cortisol in our blood, making us feel stressed. Most children carry a water bottle with them, but make sure that they're using it – sipping water can even be very calming. Encourage reluctant water drinkers by letting them choose their own cup, adding ice cubes or fruit to their drink and building drinking breaks into your routine. Teenagers might enjoy using a water-tracking app too. Very weak squash, home-made smoothies and water-rich foods, like cucumber and strawberries, can add variety to your child's fluid intake.

Improve
their sleep

Help your child to get the best night's sleep possible with a good bedtime routine. Poor sleep and late nights exacerbate stress and can get mornings off to a difficult start. You could include a relaxing bath, a warm drink and a pre-sleep meditation or quiet story before bed. You might like to use muted lighting in the evening and to have a "no screens" rule in the hour before bed, as late-night screen time can stop children from dropping off. (The light from screens suppresses the production of sleep-inducing melatonin.) If your child is a worrier, help them to write down their worries or pop them in a worry jar before lights out – or suggest that they think of three good things from their day so that they go to sleep thinking happy thoughts.

Help your teen to sleep well

The body clock changes during puberty, making it harder for teens to fall asleep as early as they used to. This can make waking up for school or college a challenge. You can help your teen's body clock shift to a slightly earlier bedtime by making sure they have some exposure to daylight during the morning – taking a break outside between nine and ten o'clock in the morning, for example, can have positive results.

You can also help your teen to sleep better by recommending they cut out caffeinated drinks, and encouraging them to exercise during the day and to avoid a heavy meal just before bed. Long lie-ins at the weekend are also best avoided, as they can upset your teen's body clock and lead to a tough start on Monday morning!

Make exercise a part of your routine

We've already talked about the brilliant benefits of exercise as a mood booster, but it's such a valuable habit that it's worth thinking about how to make it a part of your long-term routine. Building exercise into your everyday activities is one plan. Could your child walk or cycle to school? Or run to the shop when you need supplies? It's also important to include exercise sessions as a regular part of your week, so that your child sees them as essential. You might want to do an activity together – jogging, swimming or martial arts classes. Lead by example and you'll enjoy the long-term benefits for the whole family.

FIND TIME FOR REFLECTION

A lovely habit to develop from an early age is to spend a little time together every evening reflecting back on your day. For younger children, sitting quietly at bedtime and simply listing what they've done can be very calming, or you could get creative and re-enact their day with their favourite teddies or toys. Encourage older children to write in a journal, make a video diary or sum up the day with a selfie. It's also nice to get everyone to relate one high point and one low point from their day once you're all home for the evening.

Read together

Studies show that reading reduces our stress levels, improves empathy, lowers blood pressure and fights depression. Getting into the habit of reading regularly with your child will set them up to enjoy these benefits for life. Read anything and everything that appeals to your child – and remember that if "chapter books" aren't their thing, there are many other ways to include reading in their day. Find an age-appropriate blog or magazine that ties in with their hobbies, encourage them to read recipes when baking or try audiobooks – they count too!

Meditate together

In a world that's packed full of sights, sounds and new experiences, we all need to sit still and have some daily downtime for the mind. In fact, studies have proved that meditation is as important for the mind as exercise is for the body. Encourage younger children to spend time sitting quietly, simply closing their eyes and focusing on the background sounds of their surroundings. There are some lovely books or recordings of meditations that will introduce your child to this wonderful calming practice. Older children may prefer apps such as Headspace, which teach the art of meditation and offer programmes for different meditative goals, including beating stress.

Create a special meditation

Try weaving your own story to help your child create a safe place to visit in their mind whenever they want to. You can tailor the details to suit them. Start by getting them to close their eyes and breathe slowly. Tell them to picture themselves somewhere safe and warm: you could suggest a setting if you like – a little cottage surrounded by snow with a log fire and a soft comfy sofa, or a high-tech space-pod, kitted out with everything they need. Get them to imagine the details of their surroundings to make it the perfect place to relax. Remind your child they can picture this safe place whenever they need to.

TEACH TIDYING

It may not sound like fun, but if you keep your home clutter-free, you'll be making life less stressful for everyone. It's easier to feel relaxed in a tidy home, and it's *definitely* easier to avoid chaotic moments searching for something essential when you're in a rush. Young children can learn to put away toys when they've finished playing. You can make "tidy-up time" fun with a song or by setting them a time challenge to get it done. For older children, make it a rule that they put school kit away as soon as they get home and tidy up the fallout from one activity before they move on to the next.

Lay down some rules

A good way of avoiding stressful conflicts at home is to establish clear rules, so that everyone knows what's expected of them. A long and complicated list will be confusing, so keep them simple. They could include:

- Tidy up after yourself

- Ask permission to use other people's things

- Don't hurt another person or their feelings...

- ... but make amends if you get this wrong

- Knock before entering someone's room

- Carry out your chores

- Don't use gadgets after ___ o'clock

Ensure children know there will be consequences if the rules are broken and discuss what these will be. You must be prepared to carry them out, of course, or they won't be effective.

Make time for a catch-up

A weekly family meeting can be a nice tradition and a safe place for everyone to come together and chat about their week. Try to make these positive events, not just a time for parents or carers to lay down the law. Keep things relaxed, with everyone sitting comfortably with a drink to hand, or have your catch-up at a family dinner or breakfast, so that it doesn't feel too intimidating. Encourage each person to say a little bit about their week's highlights and to share anything that's worrying them – perhaps you can brainstorm ideas to sort out any problems together. It's a good time to discuss and iron out any household issues too.

Embrace routines

Having a set morning and evening routine will make sure everyone is organized and minimize stressful moments with people queuing for the bathroom. If you already have a routine in place, can you improve it? Try to use cues to remind your child to do their tasks — if they have a bath in the evening, can they lay out their things for the next day while the bath is running, for example? (Teaching children to plan ahead is a very valuable lesson.) Make sure they have somewhere accessible to store everything they need, so that they can put coats, shoes and school kit away as part of their home-time routine.

BUILD IN SOME BONDING TIME

As children grow up and take on more commitments – and see their friends more often – you can find yourselves spending less time together as a family. Try to eat a sit-down meal together at least once a week and plan regular group activities or trips. Time with family is time when children can feel relaxed and accepted. Everyone will benefit from sharing moments together without chores or commitments, simply having fun and making great memories. Time together is truly something to cherish, so enjoy it!

Schedule some screen-free time

We've already talked about the benefits of a screen curfew before bed. Studies show that too much screen time in general can impair social skills and lead to low mood, so scheduling in some tech-free moments during the day can be a really positive idea. You might want to do this subtly – distracting a teenager with baking or sports, or taking a younger child out to walk the dog or help buy a present, for example. Alternatively, you could include a regular half-hour when everyone – including you! – turns off their phones and reads together or enjoys a hobby.

CHAPTER 6
Skills for Life

As you help your child deal with tricky situations – and, no doubt, deal with a few of your own – you're teaching them valuable life skills: how to problem-solve relationship issues, how to learn from their mistakes, how to adopt a positive attitude. This chapter takes a look at some of these skills and shows you how to help your child take them on board, so that they grow into stronger, happier and less stressed adults.

Learn from your mistakes

Teach children to look at mistakes in a positive way – as a learning experience – and you'll help them to avoid stress and negativity when things don't go to plan in future. The best way to teach this lesson is to demonstrate it yourself. If you mess up, rather than dwelling on things, talk about what you've learned from the experience. Similarly, if your child makes a mistake, try to focus on the positives – "You tried really hard", "Well done for giving it a go", "At least you know what to expect next time", and so on. Remind them that their heroes had to practise and fail many times before they got to be at the top of their game.

Practise positivity

A positive attitude is something you can develop through practice. People with an optimistic outlook tend to perform better at tasks, feel less stressed and – of course – get to have more fun, as they'll give more experiences a try. Cultivate positivity by seeing tricky situations as challenges, rather than trials; by using positive affirmations ("I can do it!"), and by standing like a superhero! Adopting a "high power" pose – standing tall and strong with shoulders back, hands on hips and head held high – will induce confidence and positivity.

GIVE THEM SOME RESPONSIBILITY

It can be tempting to do everything for our children; however, giving them a little responsibility can really pay dividends. Children respond well to being given ownership of certain tasks or decisions – they feel grown-up, being in control of part of their lives. By doing so you're setting them off on a path toward independence. Start small, with a few basic chores – such as putting away their clothes or loading the dishwasher – and see how you get on. If it's tricky at first, it's worth persevering: remember that your child is learning about time-management, self-discipline and cooperation. Studies show that self-sufficient children go on to be calmer adults with higher self-esteem.

Help them build positive relationships

If we're lucky, many of us build friendships in childhood that can last a lifetime. This is when we develop our interpersonal skills too. Try to guide your child as they interact with others and build positive, nurturing relationships. Walking away from an argument, thinking before they speak and getting perspective on a difficult interaction are all really important skills for your child to learn. Equally important, of course, is teaching your child when to stand up for themselves. Life will provide the lessons here, so all you can do is be on hand to help your child learn from them.

Clear up communications

Good communication skills will benefit your child every day and help them to negotiate stressful encounters when necessary. It's surprising how many adults could do with some basic conversation skills! Your child will be doing brilliantly if you can help them to learn the following:

- **to listen attentively when someone else is speaking**

- **not to interrupt or speak over others**

- **not to speak with their mouth full**

- **to be considerate and appropriate**

For older children:

- **to think ahead about what they want to say (and to say it clearly)**

- **to stand up for themselves politely and calmly**

- **to ask open-ended questions and build conversations**

Cultivate kindness

If you can encourage your child to approach others with kindness, you'll be helping them to surround themselves with positivity as they grow into adults. Studies show that kind people are happier people.* They tend to think the best of others and acknowledge that everyone has challenges in life, so they're less likely to take negative interactions to heart or spend too long dwelling on them. If we radiate kindness into the world, it spreads happiness to those around us. And, if your child cultivates kindness, they will find it easier to treat *themselves* kindly, which is very important indeed. This is something that you can instil in them whenever you get the chance.

* Source: "Very Happy People", *Psychological Science*, 2002

TEACH THEM TO BE MINDFUL

Mindfulness is so beneficial for our well-being. There are plenty of simple – and fun – mindfulness exercises you can try with your child as a great introduction to this peaceful practice. Even better, you'll find yourself feeling calmer and more grounded if you do these activities together. Mindfulness teaches us to focus on the details of the world around us and helps us to reconnect with our senses as we pause to appreciate its beauty. Children are naturally geared up for this as they're brilliant at noticing these details. You can start your child on their mindfulness journey by simply observing and chatting about the things you see around you as you go about your day.

Play mindfulness games

You can promote mindfulness with any of these activities. Once you get started you'll come up with more ideas that will appeal to your child in particular. Try getting them to:

- Focus on a favourite object and explore it using all (appropriate!) senses.

- Hunt the house for aromatic items and describe their scents.

- Do some jumping jacks and focus on their racing heartbeat and how their body feels.

- Study the design of a favourite video game or book cover.

- Prepare and taste their favourite meal, focusing on the flavours of the ingredients.

- Do a "sound scan" of their surroundings by closing their eyes and listening to all they can hear.

Prepare them for stressful situations

Helping your child to prepare ahead and do all they can to get ready for situations such as exams and school plays will help them to feel more confident and less anxious. It will also teach them how to plan ahead for job interviews or presentations in later life. You can help them to research or practise for the big day and to get enough sleep the night before. If nerves are a problem and your child has a favourite sportsperson or actor, you could find out how their role model prepares for a big match or performance and try out their tips for dealing with pressure.

Explore how emotions come and go

If your child is in the middle of an upsetting situation, it can be difficult for them to realize that they will feel more positive again soon. If you help your child to learn that emotions come and go, they should find the difficult times less upsetting. You could fill in a mood tracker together (see p. 16) and notice that down days are always followed by happier times. Another nice exercise is to watch clouds floating past and tell your child that our feelings flow by in a similar way. Sometimes there will be dark clouds overhead, but these always move on and sunny skies reappear. Teach them to sit still and observe their feelings without getting too caught up in the negative ones: just notice them and let them pass.

CALM CONFLICTS

Conflict resolution skills are a great bonus in life. If your child has siblings, you might find you have plenty of opportunity to teach this at home, but any situation where your child has a difference of opinion is a chance for them to learn. Advise your child to walk away from heated situations, to get some perspective (by talking to someone or writing down what happened) and then plan how to move on. You could tell them that it's best to clear up misunderstandings when they're calm enough to do so. Teach your child to apologize when they're in the wrong and – when they're not – to remember that other people's poor behaviour reflects badly on the person involved, not on them.

Put things in perspective

Getting perspective on a situation can be tricky, but it's a good skill to practise as it can stop stress from building up. Remind children that many situations that can seem like the end of the world at the time are often forgotten in a few weeks or even days. If your child has a specific worry, you could help them to realize that – depending on the situation – even if their worst-case scenario happened, they'd still cope and be safe, loved and happy. Perhaps they're worrying about something that's really unlikely to occur – such as forgetting everything they've revised for an exam – and you could point out that this has never happened before, to help them see that, while you understand their feelings, their fears are not likely to come true.

Teach them to acknowledge and release

Learning how to let out our feelings – rather than suppressing them – is another valuable life skill, as it can stop stress levels from rising. Help your child to find a way to release emotions safely, burning off some anger with an exercise session, or working through sadness by writing in a diary, for example. Teach them that it's important to acknowledge their feelings before letting them go. A simple way to do this is to get them to pause when they feel a strong emotion and then fill in the blanks in these sentences:

"I am feeling _____ at the moment because _____ ."

"To feel better I could _____ ."

Show them how stress affects the body

Although long-term stress is unpleasant, the short bursts of stress that your child may experience when they're facing a challenge are a natural reaction and even have a positive side to them. When we're stressed, our memory is boosted; our pulse quickens, pumping oxygen around the body, and hormones are released that help us to work speedily and effectively. If appropriate, you could help your child to see the benefits of these "special powers" preparing them for their challenge, rather than worrying about the way their body is reacting.

CHAPTER 7

Look to Yourself

Being a parent or carer can be challenging, wonderful, rewarding and exhausting – sometimes all in the space of a day! – which is why it's so important to look after yourself. This chapter includes some tips to help you focus on your self-care. It also looks at ways in which you can influence your child and how changing your own habits can help to lower your child's stress levels.

KEEP DOING WHAT YOU'RE DOING

It can feel as though you're pretty powerless when your child is struggling with a situation that's outside your control, but never underestimate the power of a hug from a parent or carer. Your child may not say it, but you're Number One to them. Simply by being on side as an ally and advisor you're already making a huge difference. So stay calm, keep the channels of communication open, and offer companionship and compassion when you can — you're doing a brilliant job.

Be a positive role model

The first person your child takes their cues from is, of course, you, so do your best to be a positive role model when it comes to dealing with pressure and emotions. Try not to get worked up about little things: if you're constantly talking about feeling stressed, your child may take on your stress. Don't try to hide your emotions during genuinely worrying or upsetting situations, though – these are opportunities for you to show your child that stress is a normal part of everyday life and to give a positive example of how to deal with it.

Watch your words

We adults don't always realize how much of our conversations children pick up on, so while it's tempting to come home and sound off about a stressful issue at work or the latest news headline, try not to do this in front of your child. Not only could they pick up on your worries, they could also make negative associations, such as "work is always stressful". Children don't have the experience to put things in perspective, so if they hear you talking animatedly about your worries, they may become concerned about these things in an out-of-proportion way. Try to discuss your challenges in more positive terms, so that your child can see that everyone faces difficulties, but they're not insurmountable.

Consider your reactions

If you miss a train, drop a bag of shopping or lose the car keys, think about how you respond before you act. This is a good opportunity for you to give your child a practical example of responding to a stressful situation in a positive way. If you need to express your frustration (in a controlled and appropriate way!) do so, but then focus on taking practical steps to solve the problem. (You could come up with a plan of action for coping with things, for example, or discuss how you're going to get some advice to sort things out.) If you can't solve it, move on rather than dwelling on something that's out of your control – another useful skill for your child to learn.

ACKNOWLEDGE YOUR MISTAKES

There will always be moments when you mess up. If you do lose your temper or say something you regret, try not to feel too guilty. Take some time out and when everyone is calm, apologize for what happened and acknowledge how your child must have felt. Discuss how you could avoid the same thing happening again and try to focus on the positives of moving forward. You will – of course – be setting your child a good example of how to behave when they get things wrong in future, so try to see that as the silver lining in the cloud.

Gather your support team

Please don't feel that it's down to you to fix everything. Building a team of helpers will ensure you get the support you need while you and your child work through stressful times together. Think of family members and trusted friends who can support you. Remember that the pastoral team at school and your doctor can also offer advice if needed. Children's charities have excellent information online about dealing with stress and your local authority may be able to provide practical support too. Any or all of these people will be happy to help, so don't be afraid to ask.

Use online resources

There's so much information out there to help you and your child through whatever you're facing. There are some good general websites to refer to (see below) and of course there are many others that focus on more specific challenges or problems. Whatever you're going through, you're sure to find someone else in a similar situation who can offer you advice and support.

- **www.apa.org**

- **www.childrenssociety.org.uk**

- **www.internetmatters.org**

- **www.kidshealth.org**

- **www.mind.org.uk**

- **www.nctsn.org**

- **www.themix.org.uk**

- **www.youngminds.org.uk**

Don't pursue perfection

While it's important to realize that you're a role model for your child, don't put pressure on yourself to be perfect, and don't feel guilty if things don't pan out the way you think they should. Remind yourself daily that you're doing the very best you can. Remember, too, that if you're constantly striving for perfection, you're not actually providing a positive or realistic role model for your child — in fact, you might end up leaving them feeling pressured to reach for impossible goals and no doubt giving themselves a hard time when they don't achieve them.

LOOK AFTER YOURSELF

It's obvious, but essential, that you need to look after yourself properly so that you can face the challenges of parenthood with as much energy and enthusiasm as possible. If you're not eating or sleeping well, you're likely to feel under par and get stressed yourself when it comes to dealing with everyday challenges. Get as much good quality sleep as you can and avoid looking at screens before bed – yes, that rule applies to you as well as your child! Make sure that you're eating properly too: think ahead and prepare healthy snacks to get you through hectic moments without resorting to sugary foods that can affect your mood and cause energy dips.

Do something that's just for you

Remember to connect with – and continue doing – the things you used to love before becoming a parent, even if you have to adjust the way you do them for the time being. It can be really tricky to do this – particularly if you have small children – but beg, steal or borrow 15 minutes' hobby time and the benefits will boost you through the week. We feel calmer and happier when we do the things we love. Connecting with your favourite activity will help you to stay in touch with your sense of self too. You'll return to your parental role with topped up levels of energy and joy, so everyone will feel the benefits.

Practise self-care

Parenting is tough and it's all too easy to neglect yourself while you get on with day-to-day family life. It's just as important that adults – as well as children – practise mindfulness or relaxation every day to safeguard their mental health. This is essential for your well-being, but you'll also be a calmer and happier parent if you include this time out for yourself on a daily basis. So whether you take five minutes sitting outside and listening to the sounds of nature or put on some headphones and listen to a relaxing track, make sure you include a mindful break somewhere in your schedule.

Pick a parental pick-me-up

If you've only got 10 minutes to yourself, here are some things you can do for a speedy self-care session:

- Sit outside, close your eyes and focus on taking deep, slow breaths, while listening to the sounds of the world around you.

- Create a calming corner away from everyday clutter and enjoy a warm drink there.

- Enjoy a short burst of exercise – either a jog, a speedy walk round the block or a dance around the kitchen.

- Have a chat (or gossip!) with another adult – preferably one who makes you laugh.

- Spend 10 minutes working towards your dream – writing, studying, training – or even just dreaming about it!

AND FINALLY...

- Be kind to yourself – remind yourself that you're doing a great job.

- Celebrate the brilliant things you've achieved since becoming a parent.

- Remember that the little things are the big things – hugs, smiles, kind words.

- You're not alone – there's a team of people out there to help you face each challenge.

- You can't protect your child from stress, but you can teach them how to handle it.

- It is absolutely possible to help your child to overcome stress and anxiety.

Conclusion

I hope that this book has shown you that, together, you and your child can tackle their feelings of stress and help them to feel happier and more confident. Even in the trickiest of times, your support and understanding will go a long way to helping them overcome their worries. Any effort that you make to help will be appreciated. Your child is being brave in facing their worries and you are being brilliant by helping them to do so.

I hope, too, that this book has reminded you that you're never alone in facing the challenge. The amount of support and information available to you is huge and ever-growing, so don't be afraid to reach out and access it. Stay strong, and remember: stop, breathe, think, act. You can do it.

Notes

Have you enjoyed this book?

If so, why not write a review on your favourite website? If you're interested in finding out more about our books, find us on Facebook at **Summersdale Publishers** and follow us on Twitter at @Summersdale.

Thanks very much for buying this Summersdale book.

www.summersdale.com